# ACCESS GRANTED

## THE V.I.P. PRINCIPLE

### 2ND EDITION

ALETHA C. WARREN & TIFFANY C. WATKINS

ISBN13 978-1-7345273-1-5

Printed in the United States of America.

Rev Media Publishing
PO Box 5172
Kingwood, TX 77325

www.revmediapublishing.com

# Dedication

This book is dedicated to our grandmothers, Pearl "Mama Pearl" Young and Willie Mae "Madea" Ceaser, for all of the prayers, love, and belief they invested in us. Your legacy lives on through our writing, our speaking, and our being.

We love you!

# Acknowledgments

We would like to acknowledge God for giving us the vision and passion to bring Access Granted into fruition. We would also like to say a grand thank you to our mothers, Loretta Watkins and Shirley Warren, who have played a great role in our becoming the successful women we are today. We would also like to thank the late Dr. J'Ramando Horton, you have stretched our minds beyond imagination, thank you for your time and obedience. You are loved and missed!

In addition, we would like to show our appreciation to all those who invested in us from the beginning: Sallie Holsey, Jim Bittenger, Felicia Thomas, Virginia Jones, Jim Stephens and Violet Colegrove, Karen Robinson, Jeremy and Jennifer Foster, and all our family and friends. We love and appreciate you for trusting in our vision, even when you could not see it.

# Endorsements

"Aletha Warren and Tiffany C. Watkins have written a clearly articulated plan for taking the steps which will lead you further along on the path you desire to walk. The steps are easy, but they are not simple! You will finish this savvy book inspired to set the intention for your goals and begin immediately to do the things needed to fulfill them. You will also be able to understand more clearly who God has created you to be and how you can fulfill his best for you in order to make a positive contribution to our world."

**Beth Misner, author of Jesus and the Secret: Where the Word of God and the Law of Attraction Intersect. www.BethMisner.com**

"Don't let the size of Access Granted fool you. This little gem, written by two leading speakers has the potential to awaken the best in you."

**—Marci Shimoff, *NY Times* bestselling author, *Love for No Reason* and *Happy for No Reason***

*"Tiffany Candyce and Aletha Warren are two of the most driven women I know. Their drive to succeed, while inspiring and helping others is contagious!*

**—Jim Bittinger, Managing partner at Bittenger Capital Partners**

"Aletha Warren and Tiffany C. Watkins are gifted, insightful communicators who have written a critically important book. It has been my observation that most people do not know what vision, identity and purpose is and is not. Ms. Warren and Ms. Watkins make their results-oriented principles clear, simple and easy to implement.

The V.I.P. Principle will change your life, forever. This book is a must-read for all those seeking to be a V.I.P."

**Dr. Robert Watkins**
**Kings & Priests Unlimited**
**Atlanta, GA**

"Reading this book has helped me to become 'interested' in doing something in my life again. It not only gave me the outline to discover what my purpose is; but also gave me further outlines to help me to accomplish successfully. I whole-heartedly endorse "Access Granted, the VIP principle that guarantees success"; and encourage you to take a look. Very valuable."

**Bill Campbell**
**Accomplished Author**
**Vancouver, British Columbia**

"It is not every day that we meet people who leave an impression on you that furthers your purpose, stabilizes your identity and encourages your vision. Aletha's innovative and entrepreneurial spirit and creative mindset will allow your vision to take legs and walk. Purpose is never spoken, it is always lived out. This is the power of Aletha's work and results."

**—Dr. Lakita Long, MS, PH. D**

# Contents

Introduction ........................................................................ xv

Foreword ........................................................................... xvii

Welcome to Access Granted ............................................... xix

What is the V.I.P. Principle? ............................................... xxi

The Man Who Thinks He Can ........................................... xxiii

| | | |
|---|---|---|
| **Chapter 1** | **What is Vision?** | **1** |
| | *Vision Location* | 3 |
| | *The Legendary Visionaries* | 5 |
| | *Stevie Wonder* | 6 |
| | *Writing the Vision* | 6 |
| | *The Vision Timeline* | 9 |
| | *Vision Crisis* | 10 |
| | *Vision Repair* | 11 |
| | | |
| **Chapter 2** | **The Eagle's Eye** | **17** |
| | *Learning to Soar* | 18 |
| | *The Advantage of Altitude* | 19 |
| | *The Eagle's Beauty* | 20 |
| | | |
| **Chapter 3** | **The Identity Crisis** | **24** |
| | *Identity Evaluation* | 27 |
| | *Getting to Know You* | 28 |
| | *The Power Couple* | 29 |

*The Self-esteem Factor*..................................30

*The Confidence Factor* ...............................30

*Identity Evaluation*.....................................32

**Chapter 4 The Chameleon In You** ........ **35**

*The Distinction* ..........................................36

*The Transformation* ...................................37

**Chapter 5 Me, Myself, and I** ............ **41**

*Self-Love*....................................................41

*Self-Improvement* ......................................42

*Self-Talk* ....................................................43

*Self-Examination*........................................44

**Chapter 6 Introduction to Purpose** ...... **48**

*What is Purpose?* ........................................49

*How to Know when You are not Operating in*

*Purpose*......................................................51

*Value*..........................................................51

*The Greatest Enemies Of Purpose* .................52

*The Pain of Procrastination*..........................55

*Procrastination is a disease that causes a slow*

*death.* .........................................................56

*The Power of Words*.....................................56

**Chapter 7 The Lion within You** .......... **60**

*Learn How to Function in your Domain* ..........61

*Know your Environment*...............................61

*The New Jack*.............................................63

**Chapter 8   How to Activate the V.I.P.**

**Principle** . . . . . . . . . . . . . . . . . . **67**

*Purpose Summation*...........................................68

*How is Access Granted to Me?* ........................68

*The Connectors* ................................................69


Access Granted Development.................................73

About the Authors..................................................77

Bibliography..........................................................81

Quotes ...................................................................83

Bonus: V.I.P. Book of Daily Affirmations..............85

Note from the Authors...........................................93

# Introduction

We agree that you are ready. We agree that you win. You are well on your way to the journey of discovery, development, and training. Today, we begin the journey. Only you can determine how far we travel.

We are excited that you have chosen Access Granted as a stepping-stone to excellence in the desired areas of your life. There are three things we will ask of you throughout the entirety of this book:

1. Be Open: To learn more than you have previously known about yourself.
2. Be Pliable: Gear yourself up to become better and achieve more in life.
3. Be Ready: Be ready to become the V.I.P. you have always dreamed about and yet only seen others become.

By reading and applying this information, you will grasp your vision, know your identity, and live in purpose. Welcome to the place where access is granted. Welcome to the V.I.P. Principle.

Sincerely,
Life Coaches Aletha C. Warren & Tiffany C. Watkins

# Foreword

"Living the successful life doesn't happen by chance or luck."

Aletha C. Warren and Tiffany C. Watkins have spent years observing and working with people who are successful, both personally and professionally. Convincingly, the V.I.P. Principle that they have developed demonstrates that ordinary men and women who create extraordinary results—regardless of age, nationality, or education—exhibit many of the same behaviors, language patterns, and ways of living. In other words, there are things that you can do, ways to speak, and ways to be that will support you in creating the results you want in your career, relationships, finances, and health—every area of your life.

"The building blocks for living a successful life
—the V.I.P. Principle."

If you desire real success in life, if you want better, healthy, and fulfilling relationships, if you want meaningful work and a deeper connection to your spiritual life—in short, if you want to live an extraordinary life—a deeper understanding of the V.I.P. Principle is crucial. Even a small improvement in the understanding and application of this powerful principle will make a huge difference in your life experience. That is the purpose of this book.

## "Life is simple. That does not mean it is easy."

Living a successful life is an important aspect of the V.I.P. Principle in achieving extraordinary human accomplishments. *Access Granted's* life coaches believe that true transformation and growth lasts a lifetime and that only *you* can do the real work of personal reflection and discovery. Only *you* can take informed, positive action that will actualize meaningful, productive change. Only *you* can discover and evaluate the underlying self-limiting beliefs, attitudes, and behaviors that prevent you from living the life you were born to live. *Only you.*

Experience your successful life today by studying the V.I.P. Principle.

*Vision, Identity, Purpose*

No matter how dark things are or become in your life, activate your sights and see beyond the impossibilities. Always see the possibilities because they are always there.

The late Dr. J'Ramando Horton
Founder, Bentley Coaching Institute

# Welcome to Access Granted

John had dreamed all of his life of traveling alone in the indigenous forests of South Asia. After a series of years, his children had become married with children of their own, his wife had passed, and he found himself in a place where he could make his dream a reality. Standing at the foot of the forest with his backpack of water, a compass, and food, he noticed a tree. It was a beautiful tree that had a distinguished, brownish-gold bark with lush green leaves. He decided to carve his initials in the tree as a memoir that he had been there; that his dream had finally come true. Then John began his journey.

With every few miles, John checked his compass to ensure he was traveling in the right direction. As he moved closer and closer to what he thought would be the end of his journey, he came upon a tree that reminded him of the tree he saw at the beginning of his journey. As he got closer to the tree, he noticed his initials. His journey had led him back to the beginning! A frustrated John looked down at his compass to ensure that it was working. John vehemently opened his backpack and found his compass instructions. As he read them, he discovered that he had not programmed his compass properly. His failure to program it resulted in a wasted, pointless journey. He no longer had enough food and water to reach his destination. A disappointed John returned home with an unfulfilled dream due to his own negligence of one thing—failure to read the compass manual.

Have you failed to read your compass manual? Have you arrived at a destination in life, unsure of how you got there or where you were actually going? Many of us are like John with unfulfilled dreams, goals, and still at the same points we began.

Or maybe you have lived your life dreaming, unsure of how to make your dream a successful reality. If this is the case, this material is for you.

The V.I.P. Principle has been tested and tried with clients from all walks of life; from corporate executives to stay-at-home mothers. The goal of the material that you are reading is YOU. You fulfilling your destiny and finding out what journey you need to pursue to achieve your goals. This manual will serve as the instruction manual to your compass and help to guide you into the fulfillment of your dreams.

The V.I.P. Principle will provide you with the practical guidance in developing the specific competencies and awareness that will be beneficial to both your short and long-term success. Our partnership will ensure that you make it to your desired goal; be it successful business owner, excelling student, better parent, or just an overall more fulfilled life. Now is the time! Grasp your vision, know your identity, and live in purpose.

So the journey begins, compass in hand. We will be your tour guides. This is your instruction manual for the compass of your life. Are you ready? Let's go!

# What is the V.I.P. Principle?

What does V.I.P. stand for? It's an acronym for vision, identity, and purpose. We are going to show you how to maximize these three areas in order to revolutionize your life. These principles focus on vision location, identity evaluation, and purpose summation. In the chapters to come, we will give you the details that will allow you to disseminate each principle with a practical approach, thus enabling you to gain the upper hand in life.

The V.I.P. Principle is likened to having special treatment. Have you ever been in the VIP section at a concert? A press box? Courtside seats at a basketball game? If you have, congratulations! You now understand the concept of the V.I.P. Principle. If you have not, you are about to experience what it is like to have preferential treatment and be admired among your friends. By reading and applying these tools, you will gain access that will guide you to a higher standard of living. That is the V.I.P. Principle.

The V.I.P. Principle will give you the keys you need to gain access to the places in your mind and life you never thought were possible. Let us explain:

If you have ever been to a high security building, you know that you cannot enter the facility unless you have an access card. Once the card is properly inserted into the identification machine, the computer will read "Access Granted."

To take it a step further, if you were to go into a more highly secured facility, you would need your fingerprints to access certain areas that common or other unqualified personnel are not allowed to enter. You would have to enter a code, place your fingerprints on the computer, and once confirmed, the computer will read "Access Granted".

The same is true with the V.I.P. Principle. Knowing how to activate specific competencies in your life will expose you to things you could only imagine.

The V.I.P. Principle will cause you to leave your fingerprints in this world. You will not only leave a legacy for your family, but you will leave a lasting impact.

# The Man Who Thinks He Can

If you think you are beaten, you are;
If you think you dare not, you don't.
If you'd like to win, but think you can't,
It's almost a cinch that you won't.

If you think you'll lose, you're lost,
For out in the world we find
Success begins with a fellow's will;
It's all in the state of mind.

If you think you're outclassed, you are.
You've got to think high to rise.
You've got to be sure of yourself before
You can win the prize.

Life's battles don't always go
To the stronger or faster man;
But sooner or later the man who wins
Is the man who thinks he can.

Walter D. Wintle

# 1

# What is Vision?

What is vision? Is it simply physical sight? Is it hindsight? The answer to each of these questions is yes and also no. Let's explain.

Vision has a dual definition. Physical sight is the process, power, or function of seeing through the eyes. Within physical sight, there is 20/20 vision, which is the ability to see both close and distant objects clearly. There is nearsightedness, which is the inability to see distant objects clearly, while being able to see things clearly within close proximity. Lastly, there is farsightedness, in which distant objects are seen clearly but near objects appear blurry. While these three types of vision exist in the natural sense, the same is true in the sense of inward vision. Let us explain.

The second definition of vision can be expressed in the terms of mental images, dreams, and imaginations; this is what we call "inner vision". Physical sight along with inner vision is having a balanced outlook on life. You have a fresh, crisp perspective, and can see where you want to be. You may not necessarily know how to get there, but you are looking and working toward the goal. Inner vision nearsightedness is to be clear on how to take action, but unclear of where you want to see yourself in the future. To be farsighted is to be certain of your future goals, but unclear of the steps to reach those goals.

Vision, as it concerns the V.I.P. Principle, is the ability to think about or plan the future in conjunction with the imagination. It is a mental image of what the future can or will hold. It is the ability to see with one's heart and emotions without using the natural senses. By far, it is one of the greatest components of the human experience. Vision is the car that, if driven correctly, will lead you to your appropriate destination in life. With any car, if the driver is not educated on the laws of driving, it is headed for destruction. Or if you are driving under the influence, you are bound to take the wrong turn, end up at an unplanned destination, or worse. Are you driving this car called vision? If so, how is your driving?

The V.I.P. Principle will provide you with the roadmap that will help you get to your destination. We cannot promise that there will not be challenges along the way. However, we do promise to give you the tools you need to overcome them.

A challenge is a task or situation that tests one's ability, and presents the opportunity to sharpen one's experience no matter the situation. Some people think of challenges as a negative, when in actuality, they can be the greatest disguised assets if approached with the right motives. Challenges help us understand what we have, how we believe and if we have what it takes to make things happen. An example of a great outcome of a challenge would be the writing of this book. When my business partner and I, Tiffany Watkins, began to write this book, there were many obstacles;

finding the right publisher, finding the finances, making time to write, etc. Though we could have taken the negative route and allowed those obstacles to deter us from completing this book. However, when we thought about all of the lives that would be changed by our tested principles, we knew that this project was bigger than us and had to see it into completion.

In life there will be many situations and challenges that come your way, just remember not to give up. There are people waiting to hear what you have to say. If we can help one person change their life for the better, it was all worth it. So, remember when you are pursuing purpose, it's always bigger than your immediate outlook.

## The V.I.P. Principle is the ability to think about or plan the future in conjunction with the imagination.

## Vision Location

Why vision location is important

Vision location helps you identify where you are in regards to destiny. Sometimes, people believe they have one destination in life, when in fact they have more. This causes major delays in reaching purpose. Vision locations are a technique we use with our clients that help us assess their current location with the purpose of navigating them to their destination. In essence, if we surmise that the client has reached a plateau or dead end, we help them devise a plan, or make necessary amendments in a current plan for progression.

Below, you will find an assessment to help you gauge where you are in regards to knowing and operating in vision. It is imperative that you know as this enables you to live a life of fulfillment on purpose.

In order for us to be effective visionaries, we must first locate the condition of our vision. The way that we do this is to present a scale from 1-10.

- 1 represents a person with no vision. This means that through a series of events, life occurrences, etc. you have lost sight of your dreams and aspirations. You feel you no longer have the ability to imagine. This is the "Dream Deferred".
- 5 represents a person that has vision, yet no application. Their reality causes boundaries and limitations, which causes an inability to think beyond the present circumstances. This is the "Dream Sluggard".
- 10 represents a person that has a great understanding of what it is to dream and make it happen, even if they have not yet achieved it. This person is fueled by vision, motivated by results, and driven by passion. This is the "Dream Maker".

1-4 represents a person with little or no vision
5-9 represents a person with a vision, yet no application
10 represents a person that has a great understanding.

You have just identified where your vision lies. No matter what number on the scale you represented, you are further along than most because you know where you are! Knowing this helps you get to where you desire to be. Remember, revelation leads to transformation. This is the first step to the train of destiny. ALL ABOARD!

## The Legendary Visionaries

Helen Keller stated, "I'd rather be physically blind than have sight with no vision." She knew the power of vision. Many consider natural sight the governing authority of their lives, thus abdicating their internal vision. As a result, goals, the ability to achieve, etc. are abandoned. Helen knew that her inability to have physical sight was a disadvantage, yet to have physical sight with no vision was an even greater disadvantage.

Ms. Keller was a great woman who suffered a childhood disease called Scarlet Fever which rendered her blind, deaf, and mute by the age of two. However, through a series of life-impacting relationships and belief in herself, she overcame her physical disabilities, which was the fear of failure. Helen pursued a life of vision becoming an author, speaker, and philanthropist. She also spent great time aiding the American Foundation for the Blind. Now, that is the impact of vision.

Helen Keller represents a legendary visionary without natural sight, yet the ability to envision and execute despite all obstacles. Circumstances and life experiences are never a reason to stop dreaming or envisioning one's self in a particular place. ***Our history reveals that battles fought without a visionary, are battles lost.*** One must see their future on the canvas of their imagination in order to make a vision into a reality. From Starbucks coffee to Apple computers, it all started with a vision. The vision gave birth to the idea. Take the time to formulate a picture on the canvas of your imagination. If you have never done it, take a simple idea or plan and visualize it. Then, keep playing it over in your mind until your heart believes it.

## Stevie Wonder
|||||||||||||||||||||||||||||||||||||||||||||||||||||||||||||||||||||||||||||||||||||||||||||||||||||||||||||||||||||||||||||||||||||

Although Stevie Wonder was not born blind, through a series of events, this world-renowned musician lost his physical vision as an infant due to too much oxygen in his incubator. However, visual impairment did not affect his ability to have internal vision.

Today, although Stevie Wonder cannot see with physical vision, he undoubtedly utilizes the greater vision—internal vision. With it, he has been able to produce countless hits and affect many lives with his music. How is this so? He was driven with a deeper desire, and responded to this desire with his natural talents. His music tells us so. He wrote, played, and arranged music out of his heart, passion, and experience in the world. He used his natural outward gifts to express his internal vision. This is why he is a legendary visionary.

In essence, internal vision is the driving force that gives meaning and fulfillment to your life and to the lives of those around you.

## "I'd rather be physically blind than have sight with no vision." – Helen Keller

## Writing the Vision
|||||||||||||||||||||||||||||||||||||||||||||||||||||||||||||||||||||||||||||||||||||||||||||||||||||||||||||||||||||||||||||||||||||

Writing one's vision is truly underestimated. Many individuals we have encountered have never written down their goals. Of the ones who have, many have resolved their goals to antiquated journals or grade school dreams, never to be revisited. It is very rare that we encounter people that keep their goals on paper and in view. This is alarming, as history informs us that goal setting is a key in achieving success. An ancient text has revealed this truth and we have found it to be evident in our lives and the lives of our clients:

*"Write the vision and make it plain on tablets, that he may run who reads it. For the vision is yet for an appointed time; but at the end it will speak, and it will not lie. Though it tarries, wait for it; because it will surely come, It will not tarry." Habakkuk 2:2-3*

In essence, the text affirms that writing down a vision is the beginning of the process that leads to success. While it is only a first step, it is an imperative step, as all other steps are built on it. The passage also affirms a three-step process that accompanies all visions:

1. Write the vision
2. Make it clear, "plain" and precise so that those who can, and are willing to assist you with it can understand it. There are individuals who will assist you in fulfilling it, but they must first have a clear understanding of your vision.
3. Wait for it. Be patient. Do not be in a rush, forgoing all necessary lessons and necessities needed for a successful outcome. Being impatient may get you to your destination faster, but may cause irreparable damage due to not obeying the rules of the process. Process is the key in the entirety of vision. Committing to your process of writing,

patience, and process will ensure that the birthing of your vision will be healthy.

This all begins with writing the vision. This is the foundation of the birth of your vision. When you write it, as you look at it daily you will begin to rehearse it and reaffirm it to your mind and belief system that it is real. This is imperative for your belief system which is the fuel to drive your vision. Every vision has a "birthday," a day for its full arrival and manifestation into this world. This text is reminding us that there is an appointed time for one's vision to come to pass. Do not get weary, it WILL happen. It says "in the end it will speak," meaning that when you write it down, it will happen. Though it may not come when you think it should, wait on it, prepare for it, and rehearse your success before you have it because it will "SURELY COME". This is a timeless principle that happened in the lives of many individuals today that changed lives throughout history. It's time for you to make history...don't you think?

It is a known fact that people who write down their visions have over an 80 percent success rate of achieving them than those who do not. People who write their vision and articulate it to the correct people often find themselves in the right situations with opportunities to help fulfill the vision. Those who see the vision within, more readily recognize opportunities that cause them to move in the direction of their goals. Here are some facts:

- 80% of people never set goals for themselves.
- Of the 20% of the population that does set goals, roughly 70% fail to achieve the goals they have set.

- Of the 20% that do write down goals, only 20% regularly review them.
- 3% of the American population sets goals consistently and are among the wealthiest people in the country.

In order to avoid the pitfalls of these statistics, the V.I.P. Principle requires goal setting to attain the above-average side of life. VIPs set goals and make adjustments when needed in order to stay on track. Life happens, but this never stops a VIP. They are motivated. They are not lazy. And when life happens, they regroup and get back to business.

## The Vision Timeline

To accomplish any goal, it is imperative to see it with your mind (mental image), your heart (imagination), and your eyes (on paper). Therefore, a Vision Timeline is necessary. A Vision Timeline is a chart that captures what you see in your mind and reflects it on paper. This will help you to prioritize things in an orderly fashion, setting a timeframe as your guideline. For instance, if you are starting a business, creating a business plan might be the first thing on your agenda. A deadline would be set in order to strive for a realistic completion date. The timeline would organize the process and keep you accountable and on track to achieve the goal. (See Chapter Review 1, for instructions on how to create a Vision Timeline.)

With a Vision Timeline in place, you are sure to see results. Commit to it. Remember that the most successful people in our world set goals and meet them. Why shouldn't you be in the league of VIPs?

# Vision Crisis

There is a vision crisis going on in our society. Fewer and fewer people are losing faith in vision and settling for whatever is available at the moment. Here are five various types of categories people get stuck in:

Type 1: Some people have been working so long for money, they forgot what vision looks like.

Type 2: Some people don't know what it's like to have a dream, therefore forfeiting what they could become.

Type 3: Some find themselves working towards their ultimate goal and get lost in the shuffle.

Type 4: Some have thrown their dreams away and are in survival mode.

Type 5: Others have the belief, but just don't know how to attain it.

These are just a few of the categories that are out there. Of the youth we encounter, many embody this truth. Their vision starts and ends with the next big singer, rapper, athlete or actor. All they know is these people are making money and living a life of luxury. We let them know that money does not rule the world, but ideas, concepts and strategies do. As we restore the vision back into our youth, young adults, and mature adults as well, we need your help by starting with you. You make the difference!

In many cases, it is most difficult for people to believe they can achieve what they once imagined or have seen others do. Life has happened which in many cases causes dreams to fade to the background in contrast to a very present reality. Reality is much easier to believe. In this case, a simple technique is used to help repair vision. Committing to this technique helps to disarm mindsets and beliefs that oppose your success. The steps are as follows:

1. sign it: Write a list of 10 "I will" statements in regards to your vision. For example: I will have a business consulting firm or I will get my degree in psychology. Commit to it by signing your signature at the bottom of the document. Keep it in a place where you can see it often.

   I will…
   I will…
   I will…
   I will…
   I will…
   I will …
   I will …
   I will …
   I will …
   I will …

2. say it: You must reaffirm to your belief system what you want to do. When you do this, your belief system joins forces with your mind and affirms that you can do it!

3. see it: You must see the picture on the canvas of your imagination and visit the picture often. It is a simple

practice of imaging and mentally meditating on your goal. You also need to place pictures of people who already are where you want to be.

Once you sign it, say it and see it…you are on your way to repairing what life, situations, etc. has torn down. Remember, you can never be at a disadvantage. Most things in our lives that are broken can usually be repaired. However, there are those things that cannot be repaired, in that situation you have to find the beauty in it and adjust to your "new normal".

# CHAPTER 1 REVIEW

Vision Questions:

What is your vision?

_____

_____

_____

What do you envision yourself doing for the rest of your life?

_____

_____

_____

Write down 3 or more of your past or present visions you never thought you could accomplish.

_____

_____

_____

Do you believe you can accomplish this? If so, how?

_____

_____

_____

Create a vision timeline. Indicate how long it will take to complete your vision. Put it in the right sequence: numbering your vision in the right order. (see worksheet at the end of review questions)

Vision Time line

❖ Let's start by listing our dreams. Start from the greatest to the least, describing in 1 to 2 sentences the purpose of that particular dream.

❖ Next, create a "vision page" for each specific dream. Label each dream at the top of the page, then make a list of the specific tasks that is needed to achieve that vision. This step transforms your dreams into visions.

❖ Create a page for each vision and label those pages "vision to execution." On each page, list the goal you want to achieve, and then list the steps that need to be taken to achieve that goal.

❖ Assign completion dates to each task and step.

❖ Imagine what it is like having accomplished your goals. Imagine you are living it, seeing it, feeling it.

❖ Every morning speak your goals aloud, visualize you have already obtained your goal. Write one task you can do that day to achieve your goal…then "Just do it!"

❖ No excuses- your goal is your priority! Repeat your power affirmations throughout the say.

❖ Replace all negative thoughts with positive ones. Know that whatever you speak, you will have…no matter if it's good or bad.

❖ Journal your thoughts, barriers, solutions, emotions, successes, etc.

❖ Accountability is an important key to your success. Find a friend, group, hire a coach. Support will help achieve your goal and a lot of times prevent a lot of pitfalls.

Enjoy your successes! Make sure to celebrate your goals when you achieve them…celebrate all the way to the finish line.

**Vision Notes:**

_____

_____

_____

_____

_____

_____

_____

_____

_____

_____

_____

_____

_____

_____

_____

_____

_____

_____

_____

_____

_____

_____

**2**

# The Eagle's Eye

When speaking of vision, it would be inconceivable to not mention one of the species with the greatest vision known in the Animal Kingdom, the eagle. While human beings have a stellar sight at what is deemed 20/20 vision, eagles tend to see four to five times stronger than humans. They have the ability to see forward, slightly backwards, and sideways, all at the same time. They can see prey from a great distance in excellent detail. It is no surprise they are known in many traditions and cultures for their great strength, and much of it is due to their spectacular vision. Vision, for the eagle, is their strength.

The eagle is the perfect example of what we should strive for in our inner vision. For it is one of the most powerful birds in the sky, ruling atmospheres that we as humans can only dream of. It's been sighted that bald eagles fly above 30,000 feet. If our inner visionary could see four to five times stronger than our physical sight, we would be SUPER visionaries. Nothing would be able to stop us! This type of vision enables one to see the future (forward), the past in perspective (backwards), and our present (sideways). We would be invincible with this type of sight! We may not have the same perception of the eagle, but we sure could practice its traits.

## Learning to Soar

So how can the vision of an eagle be applied to your life? Let's take the ability to see things from far away and call that futuristic vision. It is the ability to see the strengths that you have and tie them into a futuristic picture of where you would like to see yourself. In essence, an eagle has the ability to spot its prey, focus on it, and attack from miles away. The eagle's distance from the goal does not determine whether or not the goal is attainable. As long as the goal is in view, the eagle will, inevitably, conquer all.

The same is true for human beings. We have the potential to achieve our goals as long as we can see or envision them. However, realistically, we have our lives, families, careers, and other important things that many times obstruct our view of the targeted goal. We tend to spend our lives with our views obstructed, never reaching our targeted goal. The result is an average life with some success, yet never a true feeling of accomplishment. Seeing with the eagle's eye allows one to identify and remove distractions, set goals, and find attainable ways to reach them. It's time to dust off your old buried vision, discover a new one, or simply pick up where you left off. It's time to reach the targeted goal.

# The Advantage of Altitude

Altitude is the height of an object or point. For instance, if I were sitting in an audience, it would be difficult for me to see everything happening around me. However, if I were on a stage, my view of the audience would become magnified. Eagle eye vision, combined with altitude, is the ability to see a target and remove the obstacles and paradigms prohibiting you from achieving it. It is a change of perspective; a change of view. It challenges you to see from the outlook of possibility instead of impossibilities. Everyone needs to have this point of view or be around people who can help to cultivate it. It provokes you to find a way—or make one—in order to discover and achieve your goals.

As stated previously, eagles have been sighted flying above 30,000 feet. However, their usual flight distance is above 10,000 feet. It is a known fact that eagles use very little energy when flying so high. In the process of achieving goals, you reach an altitude where you will begin to have sweatless victory. Meaning things get easier and you are able to coast and enjoy the fruit of your labor. That is the point we all want to get to and it is attainable. If you can think it, you can achieve it. The only delay between your current situation and sweatless victory is belief. YOU CAN DO THIS!!!

**Seeing with the eagle's eye allows one to identify and remove distractions, set goals, and find attainable ways to reach them.**

# The Eagle's Beauty

Sometimes we allow life to become so busy and so routine that we fail to admire the beauty the world has to offer. We will start by acknowledging the beauty of the eagle. Eagles are known for how high they can fly, the span of their wings, their sight and even their longevity. Here are some areas we miss about the eagle. An eagle's wingspan ranges from 72 to 90 inches, bald eagles have 7,000 feathers, they can live as long as 30 years, they are at the top of the food chain, once paired, eagles remain together until one dies.

Wow, I know. What an awesome creation? So are you! STOP! Admire the beauty you have to offer this world. No longer allow this world, situations, or friends to define what is and what's not beauty. Beauty is in the eye of the beholder. It only matters what you think about yourself. The only reason we wrote about the beauty of the eagle is to identify the intricate parts of the eagle that people do not see. Now it's your turn. It's time to show the world the intricate parts of your life that makes you beautiful. On a daily basis, people see the outside of a person. They see how you are dressed, how you speak, your non-verbals and they judge accordingly. Take time right now and write down at least 5 things about yourself that you hide from the world. Things that make you, things that you have been afraid to show people in fear that they may not accept you. Show the world that you are different, unique, unconventional, special, and independent.

Write 5 attributes about you:

1.

2.

3.

4.

5.

Now that you have written 5 things that distinguish you from everyone else, I want you to repeat the following affirmation.

I LOVE ME, AND I ACCEPT ME FOR WHO I AM. I WILL NO LONGER CHANGE FOR ANYONE, BUT EMBRACE THE FULLNESS OF WHO I AM

(If you have to keep saying it until you believe it, do it. Remember this is ALL about YOU)

# CHAPTER 2 REVIEW

Let's get into action. Develop an Eagle Plan for your visions, dreams, and aspirations. This plan will include the following steps:

1.  Make a detailed description of your characteristics and talents.

    _____

    _____

    _____

    _____

2.  Describe how you view yourself in regards to your natural gifts, talents, and personality.

    _____

    _____

    _____

    _____

3.  Where do you see yourself in the next 5 years?

    _____

    _____

    _____

    _____

4. Provide a list of obstacles that are preventing you from reaching your goals in life on one side of your paper. On the other side, write how you plan to overcome them.

_____

_____

_____

5. How will your vision affect your personal life, emotions, finances, and community, etc.?

_____

_____

_____

**Vision Notes:**

_____

_____

_____

_____

_____

_____

_____

_____

_____

_____

_____

# 3

# The Identity Crisis

There is an outbreak of a disease that has been plaguing our nation for centuries. It is more contagious than the coronavirus. It's called the identity crisis. This disease has infected and affected many people. It does not care what age, race, or gender you are. It feeds on ignorance and attaches itself to one's dreams, visions, and hopes and destroys them all.

To have an identity means to know who you are in respect to your personality, gifts, background, past and present experiences, and embracing and appreciating them as specifically unique to you. To be in an identity crisis means that an individual is experiencing a period of uncertainty and confusion in which an individual becomes unsure of his/her self-worth, typically due to societal and or other external expectations for their lives. This definition strongly describes the state of our generation today—a generation that has found comfort living in a self-compromising state of existence.

When we think of identity, we think of something that is unique in an individual and causes them to stand out from the crowd. Identity declares who you are without having to verbally explain. It is your essence; what helps to create the core of your existence.

## Identity Crisis feeds on ignorance and attaches itself to one's dreams, visions, and hopes and destroys them all.

Typically, when asked the question "Who are you?" people tend to describe what they do in respect to a profession, talent, or role in the home. Typical answers include "I am an administrative assistant," "I am a police officer," or "I am a stay-at-home mother." Although these are correct descriptions of a particular facet of one's life, they are not accurate descriptions of who one is. They are adjectives describing what one does without ever actually touching the core of who they truly are as individuals. With this in mind, many people do not know the difference between who they are and what they do.

Once, a young man by the name of Sam was asked who he was. He replied, "I'm Sam. I'm a very creative person. I love the arts and theater." In this statement alone, Sam displays his ability to decipher between identity and occupation amongst other things. It is likely that people like Sam enjoy life at a fuller measure because their existence is not wrapped up in what they do, and as such, they are not subject to feelings of failure as a result of an unexpected change in occupation or any other supposed letdown. Essentially, their value is not attached to a thing. Therefore, many people like Sam do not feel the undue pressure of external influences. Rather, they are fulfilled in who they are as people, not just in what they do.

As life coaches, we are able to see a lot working with youth and young adults. A lot of them walk around as what seems to be zombies. The reason we say that is because they have no hope, don't believe in the future, and they only believe in the moment. However, not all youth and young adults are like that, some are very much focused and have ambitions for life. I remember going to speak to some youth in Dallas and had a chance to talk to them one-on-one, you would be amazed at the issues they face. A 16-year-old soon-to-be father not knowing how to care for a child, a promiscuous 15-year-old girl wanting to keep her boyfriend the only way she knows how... The list goes on and on, that is why we have dedicated our business to helping people grasp their vision, know their identity and live in purpose. I remember hearing a statistic that stated that every 9 seconds in America, a student drops out of school, never to return.

Contrary to popular belief, identity crisis in adults is the main cause for identity crisis among our youth. Parents pass on who they perceive themselves to be to their children, not realizing the confusion it may cause. After talking with parents, we understand the children who display misconduct in school and public. Our mission is to never expose a problem without offering a solution. The solution is going to take all of us coming together and acknowledging that there is a problem and then take the necessary steps to solving them. V.I.P. Access Granted is one of those entities that is here to help solve the problem.

# Identity Evaluation

There was a vice president, Jim, of a company that just hired an intern, Casey, just graduating from college. Casey worked closely with Jim because she was being trained by the best. She worked hard and long hours but that didn't bother her because her mission was to become a permanent employee of this great company. Jim really liked Casey and knew that she had the potential to do very well. There was only one thing Casey did not understand, when Jim was in the presence of the CEO and his colleagues, he would treat her badly. He would boss her around as if she were his secretary. He would also never introduce her to the CEO. But when Jim was alone with Casey, he was the nicest guy. Confused, Casey asked Jim if she had done anything wrong, and Jim said "No, of course not." So, Casey let it go and went home. The next day, the same thing happened again. After everyone left, Casey pulled Jim aside and confronted him about the way he'd been treating her. Strangely, Jim didn't notice. After Jim apologized, he went home and thought about what Casey said and realized she was right. That one conversation caused him to evaluate why he was acting the way he did. The next day, he apologized to Casey over and over again and thanked her for bringing that to his attention. From that day forward, he never changed who he was just to please other people.

I know you probably have experienced this, or maybe your situation didn't have such a happy ending. The moral of this story is to always self-examine YOURSELF. You don't have the time nor energy to find out what's happening with everyone around you, but you can always upgrade, and improve yourself. Note to self: it is ALWAYS good to at least have one friend in your life that will tell you the truth about you.

## Getting to Know You
||||||||||||||||||||||||||||||||||||||||||||||||||||||||||||||||||||||||||||||||||||||||||||||||||||||||||||||||||||||||||||||||||||||||

There is a path that leads to you identifying who you are. It is a component of the V.I.P. Principle called the Power, Passion, and Personality Effect, also known as P3. The first component of P3 is Power, it has to do with recognizing the thing which fuels you and gives you the strength in life to thrive. Discovering this power begins with becoming aware of your likes and dislikes, your strengths and weaknesses, and embracing them as your own.

The next "P" is Passion. It represents the discovery process of your passions as well as the things that drive you, causing you to come alive when you do them. For example: Sue is good at many things. She loves animals, but cooking is her passion. Therefore, no matter how much she tries to pursue becoming a veterinarian, there will always be a void in her life, unless she decides to follow her passion of becoming a chef.

The last "P" is for Personality. Your personality is specific to you and your designated purpose in life. It also helps to make a difference in the world as a whole. Many have sanguine, flamboyant personalities, while others are quiet and reserved. Whatever your personality type, it is important that you understand and embrace who you are as an individual. Comprehending your personality plays a role in understanding the greater purpose of your life.

Learn to find the strengths and weaknesses of your personality as well as how to utilize them in a way that brings the greatest success to your efforts.

Becoming aware and secure of your power, passion, and personality are key factors in the discovery of you.

I am sure you have heard people stereotype others who are unaware of their identity as "fake," "plastic," or "carbon copies". In actuality (and in most cases), they simply never took the time to develop their identity and understand what they have to offer as an individual. This absence of identity is the reason that individuals find themselves blending in, rather than standing out in the various arenas of life. There are many reasons for this. Environment, upbringing, and convenience—to name a few—can be hindrances to a healthy development of identity. Environment and upbringing serve as a foundation for one's belief in self. If an individual is told or given an impression in their early years or into their teens of how little they are valued, it is likely that they will believe exactly as they have been told. Discovery of self, in many cases, tends to pale in comparison with the natural occurrences of life. Therefore, the occurrences of life tend to stand in the way of many a person's discovery of identity.

Experience can also be a hindrance to understanding one's identity because it is usually the easy way out or shortcut to something. Ultimately, it will lead to an unfulfilling life.

## The Power Couple

There are many factors that contribute to an identity crisis. However, we will focus on the two most important factors which are as follows:

1. The Self-Esteem Factor
2. The Confidence Factor

## The Self-esteem Factor
||||||||||||||||||||||||||||||||||||||||||||||||||||||||||||||||||||||||||||||||||||||||||||||||||||||||||||||||||||||||||||

Self-esteem is how you assess your value in relation to your personal world as well as the world around you. Without healthy self-esteem, it can be very difficult to accomplish what you were put on this earth to do. The reason? Your self-esteem is tied into your personal belief system, thus affecting your decisions and ability to transform dreams into reality. Low self-esteem, as well as lack of belief in self, creates debilitating, self-defeating attitudes which make it difficult for an individual to accomplish their goals. This causes individuals to not believe that they are capable of completing their goals. This type of thinking causes a domino effect in one's life. You must understand that self-esteem is tied to so many aspects of who you are. If your self-esteem is low or non-existent, it will show up in every area of your life such as job opportunities, marriage, friendships, and more. You will find it very difficult to feel that you are worthy of the best in any of the areas listed above. Low self-esteem is like taking a journey through life with only half of a map. It will only get you so far.

## Your self-esteem is tied into your personal belief system, thus affecting your decisions and ability to transform dreams into reality

## The Confidence Factor
||||||||||||||||||||||||||||||||||||||||||||||||||||||||||||||||||||||||||||||||||||||||||||||||||||||||||||||||||||||||||||

Confidence is having the trust, belief, and certainty about yourself as well as believing that what you have to offer is valuable and unique to you. An individual who has confidence is the difference between the salesperson that makes the sale versus the salesperson that does not. People are naturally drawn to confident individuals. The reason for this is that people will buy into the idea of you before they even think about what product or service you are offering. Your confidence is a determining factor in your personal, professional, and overall success.

Confidence speaks louder than words. You are what people see in their first introduction. How you present yourself will determine how people receive you. Sometimes you must simply believe you have confidence while endeavoring to attain it. If you start practicing confidence, eventually, you will become confident.

Self-esteem and confidence go hand-in-hand. With the V.I.P. Principle, they have the greatest effect and impact, displaying itself in mind-blowing opportunities and great success. Although self-esteem and confidence can exist without the other, to operate in such a manner can create a disaster. For example, what happens when one can no longer function in a professional role that they felt gave them such value in life? Confidence is obliterated. Yet, if you allow your confidence in yourself, as well as your abilities, to be paired with your high self-esteem, it can cause you to create self-employment and open doors of opportunity beyond your imagination.

The next component, although it is not a part of the power couple, carries great weight of its own. It's your environment. Your environment can create or hinder drive in your life. It plays an important role in your self-development. There is a saying which states: "Birds of a feather flock together." If you are hanging out with people who have little-to-no vision, then it can be difficult—although not impossible—to have a vision of your own.

# Your environment can create or hinder drive in your life.

Choosing to surround yourself with people who are of great influence can challenge you to reach further than where you currently are because you are surrounded by individuals with vision who are accomplishing their goals.

## Identity Evaluation

As we have stated in previous chapters, identity is such an important subject that many ignore. We innately become influenced by our environment and the people around us. Identity evaluation helps you to pinpoint where you are in terms of your identity. Do you know who you are? Are you comfortable with yourself? Do you change or become common to be accepted? These are some of the questions we want you to ask yourself.

Make sure that the people you are surrounded by are comfortable with you being yourself. The next time you go out in a setting with friends or family, evaluate yourself. If people cause you to change for the worse, run! If people cause you to change for the better, then those are the people with which you want to build relationships. Surround yourself with people who celebrate you, not people who tolerate you. This is how you evaluate your identity.

# CHAPTER 3 REVIEW

Identity Questions:

1. Identify your self-esteem level, 1 being the lowest and 5 being the highest.

   _____

   _____

   _____

   _____

2. Name the areas in your life that you are the most confident.

   _____

   _____

   _____

   _____

3. What factors have contributed to the way you see yourself? Please be specific.

   _____

   _____

   _____

   _____

4. Describe how the P3 principle affects your life. What is your power? What is your passion? And what is your personality? Be specific.

_____

_____

_____

_____

5. If you were to evaluate your identity, what would be your conclusion?

    a.   I don't really know who I am.

    b.   I have an idea of who I am, but I am not completely sure.

    c.   I know who I am.

**Vision Notes:**

_____

_____

_____

_____

_____

_____

_____

_____

**4**

# The Chameleon In You

When referring to identity, the chameleon gives the most accurate depiction. Though most people associate the chameleon's traits with negativity, we do not; we have a different perspective. An individual might say that a person is likened to a chameleon because they are untrustworthy and "change their colors" depending on the situation or environment and this may be true for the said individual. Yet in reality, the chameleon's skin does not change because it is inconsistent; as a matter of fact, it has no control over it. It is a part of its natural chemistry. It changes to adapt to its surroundings, which consists of its emotional state, sunlight, and temperature. It is one of the most effective camouflage methods adopted by any creature. In fact, the color changes are one of the reasons that allow the chameleon to survive in any type of weather or environment.

This depiction of the chameleon could actually help you to understand the personalities of some people. I'm sure that some people, if not all, have encountered someone who seems to have multiple personalities. Not referring to a chemical imbalance but the result of bad or unresolved issues of experiences. There are some people whose personalities change when they are around certain people, some change when money comes into the picture, etc. There are tons of reasons I can state why people change, but the one common denominator would be a lack of identity. Not knowing who they are and not willing to embrace who they were created to be.

## The Distinction

You may be wondering how a chameleon can assist you in learning about your identity. Yet, by studying the chameleon, we can discover that mirroring its traits will place us on the path of discovery. This path helps you to identify who you are, what you have control of, and how you can adapt to your environment.

When discovering your identity, it is important to know your environment and how it alters or transforms you. Knowledge of this is important in learning to understand you. Discover what causes you happiness, sadness, pain, etc. The chameleon's color changes to match its emotional state and can also be is used as a defense mechanism. This simply means that sometimes we change without knowing it. This may be caused by our emotions, good or bad. You can also change by defending yourself from those who you think are attacking you for no apparent reason.

Is this the same for you? Are you aware of how your colors change depending on who enters a room? Do your actions change if you are around certain people? Our location—be it home, work, school, etc.—has the ability to affect the way we react to life and can ultimately change the outlook we have on ourselves. Our identity is molded by society, our experiences, and our upbringing, whether negative or positive. It is up to us to take what is positive, apply it to our lives, and throw out what is negative. We must change our emotional reactions and responses and never allow our situations to dictate our world.

## Our identity is molded by society, our experiences, and our upbringing, whether negative or positive.

## The Transformation

Lastly, the chameleon is known to shed every few months. You should do the same. Set aside a time where you can have a self-examination. What do you allow to define you? Who are you? People respond to you based on how you view yourself. A bully only bullies when they know the victim does not understand their identity and therefore, will not fight back. It's time to fight back. It's time to know, respect, and declare your identity to the world, and most of all, to you.

Don't allow your situations, people or things to "bully," in-timidate, or convince you to be different than you are organically. Whatever you do, don't allow them to change who you are. Let me give you a few examples of what we mean:

1.  Situations – when problems or obstacles come, the way that you don't allow them to bully you is to not give those situations your power. Your power could be your emotions, your attention, etc. If you take on the mindset that you could never be at a disadvantage, this will help you change the way you respond to the things that come your way.

2.  People – people bully other people for many different reasons. It could be because of what is going on in their home environment, it could be that they once were a victim and now they have become what they were a victim of, it can also be because they have low self-esteem and don't know who they are, anger problems, etc. There are countless reasons people do what they do. Again, the way that you handle this is knowing who you are, loving who you are and not giving people your power (emotions, attention, etc.).

3.  Things - material things come and go...it's important not to allow things to bully you. Know that things are replaceable and never get too attached.

# CHAPTER 4 REVIEW

Chameleon Questions:

1. Does your personality or mood change based on your environment or certain people?

_____

_____

_____

_____

2. How do your characteristics reflect that of a chameleon?

_____

_____

_____

_____

3. Are you aware of your emotional reactions and responses to situations in your life?

_____

_____

_____

_____

4. How do you believe others view you? How do you view yourself?

_____

_____

_____

5. If someone were to do a story on your life, what would they find? Would they find the real you or a camouflaged you? Describe their findings.

_____

_____

_____

**Vision Notes:**

_____

_____

_____

_____

_____

_____

_____

_____

_____

_____

**5**

# Me, Myself, and I

## Self-Love

Have you ever heard of the saying "you can't love someone else until you love yourself"? Well, it's true. Though we do it all the time. When we don't love ourselves, we usually mask it by trying to love someone else. What we're really doing is giving a false sense of love, trying to give someone something that you yourself don't possess. From that, a couple of things can happen.

1.  you become overly obsessed with this person because they now define who you are.
2.  you really cheat the other person from knowing the "whole" you because you don't know the whole you. Self-love is really important, it's important that you love who you are, your differences, what makes you YOU! If you

don't love or respect yourself, others won't either. People treat you how you treat yourself.

Now that you know what it is, let me help you to apply tools to help you to begin loving yourself. First, get to mirror and look at yourself from head to toe and begin to tell yourself that you love every part of you, flaws and all. This is a technique we use with our clients called "mirror time." You take off the make-up (for the women), all the hats you wear throughout the day and deal with the real you. A motto that we use in V.I.P. is "whatever you don't like, change, and whatever you can't change, find the beauty in it." Now, this doesn't mean go out and distort your body by adding to it. An example of what we mean is: if you feel you need to lose a few pounds, eat right and exercise. If you feel you are lonely, go out and find a social group to visit, etc. Those things are easy to change.

Self-love is the most powerful attribute you can have…we can walk up to any person and there's always something they would like to change about themselves, but finding a person who loves themselves is really rare. Make up your mind today to be that person, don't allow society to tell you who you are and what beauty is. You tell them what beauty is by being YOU…authentically YOU!

## Self-Improvement

This is a timeless principle, we are always working to improve ourselves, if we're not…we should be. Self-improvement is essential for growth. In order to grow in any area of your life, it requires that you improve in that specific area. Sometimes we can be hard on ourselves and see the glass half empty instead of half full. Which means, instead of appreciating the things we have accomplished in our lives, we usually focus on the things we have not accomplished. A balance is needed. It is great to set goals and it is even better to celebrate those goals once you achieve them. Self-improvement can be seen as the stairs to success, as you take one step at a time, you are closer and closer to your goal.

If your goal is to become greater than you are now, it's time to improve yourself. Make it so that you are invaluable in whatever arena you choose. The way you do that is by educating yourself in that field, surrounding yourself with the right people, people who would add positivity to your life.

To help with self-improvement, there are books, seminars, the internet, libraries, etc. to help you. Remember, self-improvement can only add value to your life, whether it's professional or personal.

## Self-Talk

Talking to oneself can be seen as "weird" or "crazy," but let me assure you that is not the case. This type of self-talk is actually very beneficial. It is the ability to encourage yourself. Sometimes we don't have the support base that we need, so we have to encourage ourselves. Though that is not always the case, this is a practice that has been used throughout history. This is an example of what self-talk is:

"Today, I am going to have a great, productive day. I will supersede my manager's expectations of me. I am the best employee in this company. I will close the most deals today…"

Now, this is a great way to start off the day. If necessary, use self-talk throughout the day. For example, if someone makes you upset, take a break, walk away, and use self-talk. Say to yourself, "I can't allow people to make me upset. When I allow others to make me upset, I give them too much power, and I control me, they don't." Self-talk has gotten us through a lot of meetings, situations with friends and family. Sometimes it's good to take a break from things and then come back after you have calmed yourself down. We strongly suggest self-talk on a daily basis. You will find that things are not as serious as we make them.

## Self-Examination

Last, but certainly not least. It is paramount to ALWAYS self-examine oneself. The only way you can really become a better person, employee, wife, husband, student, etc. is to constantly re-evaluate where you are. Self-examination helps you to look closely at your motives, conduct and actions in everything you do. To achieve personal excellence you must keep tabs on your thoughts, emotions, and behavior. A good practice to have is: at the end of the day, evaluate your day and your decisions. That will help you to see where you can improve, and the next day you have an opportunity to start all over.

Self-examination also helps you to dispel limitations that you and others have put on you. Without self-examination, limitations tend to take over. It's easy to become what people think you should or shouldn't be. However, when you examine yourself, it's easy to locate what you want for yourself and what others want you to be and make the distinction.

I must warn you there is such a thing as "too much" self-examination that can cause you to become really frustrated and bitter. You want to steer away from that. The way you do that is to have a mentor or friend that you can talk to and help you find the balance. Watch out world, you are on your way to becoming a better YOU, you can do it!

Self-love, self-improvement, self-talk, and self-examination are all used to locate your identity. If your identity was a blank canvas, these traits would be the paint you use to begin the process. Use each one of these areas to create a masterpiece. One day at a time, one step at a time, don't try to do it all at once...it will make you frustrated. It's time to hang your personal masterpiece in the art gallery of life. People are waiting to invest in you, you are invaluable!

# CHAPTER 5 REVIEW

Me, Myself &I:

1. Name 3 things you love about you:

   _____

   _____

   _____

   _____

2. Name 3 areas that you would like to improve about you:

   _____

   _____

   _____

   _____

3. Write a "self talk" phrase that will assist you in frustrating moments:

   _____

   _____

   _____

   _____

4.  Write a paragraph on personal self-examination. Take the time to assess what you have discovered and how it has affected you and those around you.

_____

_____

_____

5.  If you were to take a truthful look into who you really are, would people like you? Would you like you? If, not ...let's change it.

_____

_____

_____

**Vision Notes:**

_____

_____

_____

_____

_____

_____

_____

_____

_____

# 6

# Introduction to Purpose

Everyone on this planet was born with a specific plan and purpose for the world. There is no other reason for the differences we all share. From personality to various levels and types of intelligence, we were all created to fulfill a plan in the grand scheme of time. What was a perfect fit for Mother Theresa was not for Babe Ruth. Can you imagine Mother Theresa in a baseball uniform, running towards home base? Or Babe Ruth in a nun's habit serving the poor in Mogadishu? Or even Donald Trump attempting to sing a Billie Holiday classic? It's kind of funny when you think about it.

It's funny because each of the individuals mentioned are lauded celebrities in their respective arenas. Babe Ruth is known as one of the greatest ballplayers in the world, while Billie Holiday was a premier jazz singer, establishing what we now know as the musical term "scatting."

So what made these people experts in their field? Why does the world deem them as the G.O.A.T. (Greatest Of All Time) in their given industry of sports, music, etc.? It's because they functioned in their God-given purpose.

It is common for people to confuse purpose with destiny. However, they are two very different things. Purpose, as stated above, is what you are born to do in this world. Destiny is where you end up as a result of the decisions you make in life. So, can you alter your destiny? Yes, you can. You can make one wrong decision that will cause you to go in a completely different direction than you are meant to go. Can you reverse destiny? Definitely, when you change your decisions you change your life. In essence, one must be very careful when making life decisions…they can affect your destiny. Here is a practice that will help with decision making: Take at least 24 hours, weigh the pros and cons and make a decision based on how it will benefit you for the best.

## What is Purpose?

When the Creator thought of you, there was an intended plan; a mission for your existence. Your natural passions, desires, and interests point to that plan. These things combined, are known as purpose.

Purpose is an area of specialization wherein you receive the greatest satisfaction out of life because you are operating in the area that was designed just for you. Many people never discover this area and for that reason, live average lives, never truly finding what makes them happy in life. Purpose is the place designed for you to thrive, enjoy life, and even make money, from doing what you are naturally gifted to do.

## Purpose explains itself. It has its own language; its own heartbeat. It thrives.

In the Michael Jackson movie This Is It, Michael was instructing a musician on a particular song. They were not seeing eye-to-eye. The musicians were not performing the entrance of a song to Michael's approval. One of them asked Michael to cue the entrance for the band. He informed the musician to simply watch him because he would just feel it. Michael was fluid with the music to a degree where it could not be made into a science or even an art for him. It was simply a part of him. It was a feeling; a feeling and a knowing.

Michael was so well-acquainted with his purpose that he could feel the music from his head to his toes and throughout his soul. Music was Michael's purpose. And just as Michael, when you are in purpose, you know it. You feel it, and others can too. There will be an audience of listeners and participants waiting for you to operate in that gift, whether it is finance, leadership, or styling hair. People are waiting for you to know your purpose. Most of all, you are waiting on you to know your purpose. You must invest the time and resources to discover it. Purpose is given by God, yet must be discovered by you.

## How to Know when You are not Operating in Purpose

How do you know when you are not operating in purpose? When you are not operating in purpose, life can become a mundane experience. Some feel lifeless or like they are caught in a routine. Here are some key indicators:

1. You genuinely do not like your occupation.
2. You dread the thought of going to your place of employment.
3. Overall, you have no sense of fulfillment in life.
4. You fill your life with activities, yet never seem to be happy while doing them.

If any of these things resonate within you, it could be a clue that you are not operating in your designated purpose. This does not mean you need to quit your job. Of course you need to make a living. Neither does it mean that you need to end a particular relationship. It simply means that it is time to re-evaluate things in your life. There is a way for you to operate in your natural gifting without compromising your financial gain or commitment to your family, friends, or other activities.

## Value

In order to understand purpose, you must understand value as well. To value you, something, or someone is to know its worth, its cost. Valuing YOU is the most important attribute you can have.

When you value you, others will as well. To help you to get a better understanding of value, I will put it in parabolic form:

Once there was a man who was on the hunt for hidden treasure, he spent many days searching for this treasure, but had no success. One day the treasure hunter came to a field, the field didn't look like much. It seemed abandoned and desolated. Though he didn't think he would find anything, he started to dig. As tired, fatigued, and hungry as he was…he continued to dig. Just when he was about to give up, he hit something solid in the ground. Thinking it was a rock, he dug around it. To his surprise, it was a chest. Inside that chest were jewels, rubies, diamonds and priceless artifacts. With great joy, he shouted and danced. Knowing the value of the field, he went back to his hometown and sold everything he had and bought that field.

The moral of the story is to recognize value. When you search for value, whether it's your personal value or finding the value in someone else, it takes time and effort. However, once you find it, your search is over and you are able to enjoy all it has to offer. Be patient and keep digging. There is much adventure to be conquered, and treasure to be found.

## The Greatest Enemies Of Purpose

Many people live their lives and never discover their overall purpose for living. Essentially, they settle for less than purposeful lives with a myriad of legitimate reasons or excuses and never abandon their current living situations. As time progresses, they remain in a stagnate way of living as the time clock of their lives continue to count down. There are specific reasons why purpose can be abandoned or aborted. These reasons are essentially the greatest enemies of purpose. They can be described in four words: distractions, disbelief, disaster and decisions.

## Enemy #1: Distractions

Distractions are issues and situations that happen in life that cause us to give our attention to them, thereby taking our attention off of pertinent things. Distractions come in many forms; people, jobs, volunteer work, relationships, etc. You cannot avoid distractions coming. However, you can avoid giving distractions too much attention. You have to understand that great fulfillment comes when you reach the goal of purpose. You have to be committed to seeing this come to pass in your life, as it directly and indirectly affects you and the people in your life. Your focus is required, without focus you lose the battle. At that time, you have detoured completely off your path. Don't allow distractions to rule you, the way you do that is to look back. Look back and see what caused you to get off track in the past, and refuse to allow it to happen again by keeping your eyes on the goal.

## Enemy #2: Disbelief

Lack of belief in self is a major enemy of success. If you deal with this, there is nothing in your way but your mindset! Disbelief is one of the greatest enemies to achieving purpose, and is the primary reason why people take a back seat and applaud the individual actually doing something about their purpose. Lack of belief in self is the primary reason people do not achieve. Lack of money and resources are NOT the reasons. Lack of belief that you can attain that money and necessary resources is a barrier. Lack of information is not a pertinent reason for not achieving purpose. In many cases, lack of initiative and aggression could be a reason. The root of this is disbelief in self that you are able to attain everything you need. The truth is YOU CAN! It is a known fact that your belief system doesn't know the difference in what's real or not real. It believes whatever you give it to believe. If you believe you are a failure, your belief system believes it and you will begin to act like a failure. If you believe you are a millionaire, your belief system takes that as fact and you attract what you are. So, NEVER underestimate the power of your belief system. Feed it the right foods and it will grow healthy, feed it the wrong foods and it will be unhealthy. If you starve it, it will die.

**Enemy #3: Disaster**

Disaster may come when one least expects it. Loss of a loved one, loss of job, or financial ruin. Many times, disaster does not give a warning when it comes to visit. Events such as 9/11 or Hurricane Ike are some examples of unwelcomed guests. As a result, we are many times left in disarray, unsure of how to continue with our lives. The truth of the matter is, if you are still living, you must continue to live. It's what we call the "new normal." It is not always easy, but it is essential that with time and adjustments that you continue to live. While heartbeat and breath are indicators of life, they are not indicators of purpose, functionality, and living. The greatest memorial to losing a loved one, losing a job, or any disaster, is to function and live life to the fullest capacity possible. Make life a beautiful legacy in honor of who or what you may have lost. Perspective also helps you to deal with disaster by being grateful that it could have been worse, and that you have another opportunity to appreciate and enjoy life.

**Enemy of success #4: Decisions**

The power of decision is one of the greatest forces in the world. Decisions have caused wars, saved lives, and have taken a life of poverty and caused great wealth and abundance. Deciding to be slothful, unconcerned, or to procrastinate is one of the greatest enemies in achieving purpose. It could be as simple as deciding to attend an event that could change your life. That event could have the capability and desire to be favorable to you. You have to decide to go after your purpose with diligence, no matter what. You have to decide to take the steps needed to achieve. Lastly, you have to decide to be committed to YOURSELF in this way…this is the greatest decision of your life. You will either make the decision to do something about your purpose, or you will decide to allow it to allude you. Your destiny is up to you, how will you decide?

## The Pain of Procrastination

Have you ever heard of these excuses: "I'll do it later, not today," or "I don't have the time"? Have you ever used these excuses? Did you ever complete that project? Let's renew our commitment to ourselves by not putting off what we can do today. Procrastination is a disease that causes a slow death. You don't notice it right away, you don't even feel the repercussions of it right away. As you look back 5, 10 or 15 years of your life, you begin to feel and experience the pain of procrastination. Things you could have and should have accomplished were never accomplished. The destination of procrastination will always lead you into desolation. Don't allow procrastination to kill your destiny, the only way you can do that is to welcome discipline into your life. Don't wait on life, because life will definitely not wait on you.

## Procrastination is a disease that causes a slow death.

What is discipline? The best way to describe discipline is to give you an example of what discipline is not. Have you ever been walking in the mall and you see a child causing a scene? The child is screaming and shouting at their parents because they didn't buy them what they wanted. The parents are trying to calm the child down, but the more they try, the louder the child gets. That is called a lack of discipline. Discipline is the ability to control or manage our behavior. It is a challenge to attain, but once you have it, many opportunities become available to you. It will make you uncomfortable, but will get you massive result. If one desires to lose weight, there are some rules that must be followed. Their eating needs to change, exercise must be incorporated into the routine. Discipline will bring you before people you never thought you would meet and places you never thought you would see. The wealth of the world belongs to the disciplined. It is a gift. Will you receive it?

## The Power of Words

The most underestimated weapon we have to annihilate ALL enemies of purpose are words. Words have the ability to create or destroy. With words we can create a beautiful life, also with words we can destroy lives as well. Life and death are in the power of what you speak. So, let's learn to evaluate what comes out of our mouths on a daily basis. When we think before we speak, we are more apt to help others. If your life were a blank canvas, what words would be used to create it?

Have you ever heard of the saying "sticks and stones may break my bones, but words will never hurt me"? This couldn't be further from the truth. I remember hearing this phrase growing up. Honestly, "sticks and stones" will heal much faster than heart wounds. When we speak to people out of hurt, anger or fear, it's like taking a match and setting a dry forest ablaze. I believe we all have been victimized by harsh words or thoughtless responses. How we choose to receive and respond will make all the difference.

Am I saying that we are responsible for what people say to us? Of course I am! One's response will either add fuel to the fire or show emotional maturity. We don't always get it right, but we challenge you to continue working on becoming the best version of yourself. Choose to speak life into every situation, and into every person. I guarantee you will become a person you're proud of and one that others look up to.

# CHAPTER 6 REVIEW

Purpose Questions:

1.  Do you have a sense of fulfillment in your life?

    _____

    _____

    _____

2.  What type of things come easy for you?

    _____

    _____

    _____

3.  What talents or skills have others consistently compli-
    mented you on in your life?

    _____

    _____

    _____

4.  What could you see yourself doing if someone said they
    would pay you to do it? Elaborate.

    _____

    _____

    _____

5. Are you practicing purpose daily?

_____

_____

_____

**Vision Notes:**

_____

_____

_____

_____

_____

_____

_____

_____

_____

_____

_____

_____

_____

_____

_____

_____

_____

_____

**7**

# The Lion within You

A lion's natural inclination is to rule its domain. They are known for their leadership, strength, and dominance in the Animal Kingdom. When a lion steps into a domain, most animals take caution. The reason? The lion is known by the species to be the King of the Jungle. A lion is a territorial animal who rules its settings, especially when pitted against other beasts.

Access Granted will cause you to discover the lion in you; that part of you that has been yearning to come out, yet never had the opportunity to do so. When we talk about the "lion within you," we are not referring to a violent side of you. However, we speak of the brevity, strength, and pride that lies within you. You must have these characteristics if you are going to survive in the world.

These are some of the keys that will grant you the access we are teaching. Now, let's open the door of destiny.


## Learn How to Function in your Domain

The lion in you is the leader that stands up when it is beckoned to operate in its domain. It is most comfortable within its natural habitat; the domain in which it was designed. It is the one who was born to lead; born to win in your given area of influence.

In the previous chapter, you learned about purpose and how to identify it. Now, it's time to reveal the lion within, in order for you to rule your domain and thrive in purpose. So what is your domain? Let's discover!


## Know your Environment

What is the area of influence you were designed to dominate? How does one practically occupy a domain? Here are three simple steps to answer these questions:

1. Know your area of purpose.

Once you know the area you were designed for, you can begin to take steps towards occupying your domain. For example, if you understand that you have a gift for working with young people, find a local organization where you can volunteer your time and become a big brother or sister. If you do not have the time, simply offer assistance when and where you are able to. But the first objective in discovering the lion within is understanding the domain in which you operate.

2. Learn how to function within a domain.

A lion's domain is where they rule and dominate. Simply put, that is what you are to do in your domain; the area in which you shine. You dominate. It does not mean that you scream to announce your presence or abilities; a lion only roars at certain times of the day. There is no need to tell the world who you are. When you are in purpose and doing what you are born to do, others will take notice and shout for you.

There are some individuals who were destined for greatness as stay-at-home mothers, while others were destined for the domain of political office. No area of influence is greater than the other. It's all about ruling the domain you are naturally gifted. No one can compete with or beat you within your appropriate setting, when you are fitting into the domain designed just for you.

3. Walk throughout your domain daily.

A lion is known to walk at least two hours a day. They tour their domain and are familiar with their surroundings. The same should be true for you. Know your area of influence and find ways to practice it daily. For instance, if you are a writer, find a way to write a paragraph or page per day. If you love to sing, sing one song per day, or study a piece of music that you enjoy. No matter what your purpose is, you can find a way to always practice it. It is your area of expertise, so own it. Discover the ways to occupy your domain on a daily basis.

For some individuals, leadership in their areas of purpose comes naturally. For others, it may be a more gradual process. Whatever your lot in life, you are well on your way to enjoying it in greater dimensions as you uncover the simplicities of a purposeful life, step-by-step. Begin to discover and uncover your purpose by setting goals and applying the Vision Timeline strategies previously mentioned. And most of all, awaken the lion within.

**Your destiny is awaiting your arrival; it is one step at a time. As you walk each step, your access will be granted.**

## The New Jack

"Jack of all trades, master of none."

Have you ever heard of this phrase? It is used to describe the individual that has many talents or endeavors, but does not have mastery of any. This term has been coined in our society by many people, and in turn, ingrained in the minds and hearts of people. Well, V.I.P. has a news flash: there is a new Jack in town! This is the Jack of many trades, master of all--- in the right season. Let me explain.

Earvin "Magic" Johnson is the best example of the new jack. One of the greatest basketball stars of all time, although not an active player at this moment, he is known for his "magic" in the arena of basketball. Basketball for Magic Johnson was the entity that opened the other doors for philanthropy, business mentorship, movie theaters, restaurants and more. But it started with one skill: basketball. The primary talent made room and financial capital for all other gifts he possessed.

With this in mind, the same is true for you! Your talent can do the same if desired. You no longer have to use only one talent, choosing the one in which others feel you are most gifted. Use the gift that is most pronounced in YOUR heart—the one that speaks the loudest to you. Choosing must not be limited to "head" knowledge, but to "heart" knowledge. If you are not sure which talent that is, continue to read this book. We will help you on the path of discovery.

Like the original "jack of all trades," you may have many skills; you may have few; some discovered, and some unlearned. But the truth is you do not have to pick your favorite and leave the other natural abilities alone. The proper thing to do is understand yourself in relation to times and seasons, when you should do certain things and leave others to rest until a given time. Trying to execute too much at once is a disaster. Take your time and develop the right gifts in the right timing, and your success will flow from there. Using the right gift in the proper timing is the fuel for your other gifts to thrive and give life to you.

Action: Go to a quiet place. Turn off cell phones and any other devices that make noise. Be quiet. Close your eyes and repeat the words: "I know what I want to do with my life." Say them over and over again for 2 minutes. Sit quietly for 60 seconds. Then, proceed with the day.

Practice this technique at least 3 times per week. In a matter of time, you will begin to identify opportunities, people, and situations that will support you with what you have been saying and meditating on. Do not allow fear, past failures, or others' opinions to deter you from what is coming your way. Embrace opportunities. You've been waiting on them...now is the time.

# CHAPTER 7 REVIEW

The Lion within Questions:

1.  Describe the Lion within you; the Leader.

    _____

    _____

    _____

    _____

2.  What is your given area of influence?

    _____

    _____

    _____

    _____

3.  How can you function in your domain daily?

    _____

    _____

    _____

    _____

4. On a scale from 1 to 10, identify the Lion within you in its current state, 1 indicating you are completely asleep and 10 indicating you are operating in your total purpose. Please expound.

_____

_____

_____

5. As a "New Jack", what would be some of the other dreams you would like to see come alive in your life?

_____

_____

_____

**Vision Notes:**

_____

_____

_____

_____

_____

_____

_____

_____

_____

**8**

# How to Activate the V.I.P. Principle

Now that you have acquired all the components of the V.I.P. Principle, you must take the final step to grant you access into the desired lifestyle you have discovered: application. Application equals activation. Application is simply the action of putting something you have acquired or learned into action. Action then translates into activation which always leads to destination. The goal of the V.I.P. Principle is to assist you in getting to your desired destiny in life.

## Purpose Summation

Summation is the process of combining things in order to create a fulfilled purpose in life. So use your Vision Timeline to bring your ideas, talents, and passions together and ultimately, arrive at your purpose. This will help you to narrow down what you excel in and are passionate about. The exercises in the Chapter 3 Review should have helped you identify exactly what passion looks like.

## How is Access Granted to Me?

Access is granted by application. You have learned how to acquire vision. You have learned how to access your identity. And you have learned how to discover your purpose. Now is the time to apply all that you have learned in order for access to be granted to your personal fulfillment in life. As a result of this fulfillment, you and all those in your life will get the opportunity to experience a new and improved you.

One thing that we encourage is for you to stay your course. Access is only granted to individuals who continue to see their goals to completion. Much of our population will not see their goals to the end, primarily because they are not willing to do what it takes, no matter the cost. You have to be determined to make the most of your life, instead of allowing life to make the most out of you. In order to do this, you must remain motivated. You must remember that you have what it takes to be on top. Most of all, you must remember that understanding and executing the V.I.P. Principle makes you a VIP in life. You will literally gain access into a world of opportunity, influence, affluence, and wealth. Welcome to our world!

So stay determined. Complete the Chapter Reviews. Rearrange your schedule to do what is needed to make this happen. Believe it or not, you are the most important person in your life. Consider the oxygen mask principle. When on a plane, the flight attendants instruct the passengers to put their safety masks on first in the event of the loss of cabin pressure before seeking to assist anyone else. Why? Because the attendant understands that if you try to assist someone else before securing your own mask, you could die.

The same is true for you as it concerns the V.I.P. Principle. You must secure this principle in your own life in order to properly enjoy your family, friends, and the world around you. Furthermore, everyone will enjoy you all the more, as you become an increasingly pleasant person. Secure your mask step by step. You will find that access will be granted to your true life and will enable others to learn from your example.

## The Connectors

Last but not least, are the connectors. Connectors can be seen as the middlemen in our lives who help to bring about the various opportunities we seek. They are the individuals who introduce us to the people or ideas we need to know in order to complete our desired goals in life. One can have more than one connector as there may be several. For example: Bill and Sue are friends. Bill is interested in investing in real estate, yet does not quite know where to start. Sue is also friends with John who is a successful real estate agent. In this instance, Sue would be the connector between Bill and John. Sue introduces the two, and as a result, not only did Bill find a lucrative real estate to invest in, he was also introduced to a great friend and connector.

The connectors play a great role in our lives. This is why it is imperative to be at the right place, at the right time, talking to the right people. With this in mind, we encourage you to meet people and network. Do not reject people because of the way they look, dress, or their seemingly low economic status. Prejudging a possible connector is the key to failure, as you never know who someone knows or how they could help catapult you into your destiny by simply making the right introduction.

We hope that you have enjoyed reading about as well as discovering the keys to the V.I.P. lifestyle in Access Granted. We hope that you will thoughtfully and sincerely count the cost and then apply the knowledge that you have gained.

## Prejudging a possible connector is the key to failure

# CHAPTER 8 REVIEW

V.I.P. Questions:

1. What 3 practical steps are you going to take to activate the V.I.P. Principle in your life?

   _____

   _____

   _____

2. How has understanding "Access Granted" changed your perspective?

   _____

   _____

   _____

3. Identify your connectors.

   _____

   _____

   _____

4. Tell us what the V.I.P. Principle is in your own words

   _____

   _____

   _____

5. How committed are you to seeing these V.I.P. Principles become a reality in your life?

_____

_____

_____

**Vision Notes:**

_____

_____

_____

_____

_____

_____

_____

_____

_____

_____

_____

_____

_____

_____

# Access Granted Development

This program is another way for you to take advantage of all the knowledge you have gained from "Access Granted, the V.I.P. Principle." We will give you keys to open up the door of your mind, to change your perspective in every area of your life. As we all know, the way companies get you to purchase their products is by repetition. We are inundated with the media; whether it's radio, T.V., billboards, internet, etc. The individuals behind the advertising industry understand that repetition is the key.

Listed below are principles to help you stay focused, achieve your goals by consistently keeping them in front of you. Use these affirmations daily. Repeat them. Continue speaking what you want to see in your life, believe it and watch results come.

## 1. MY VISION IS CLEAR.

It's very important that you are clear on what you want to do and how to make it happen. The canvas of your imagination is a great place to create a vision masterpiece with precision and clarity.

## 2. I LOVE TO SERVE OTHERS

When you decide to be generous and helpful to others, people are more apt to come back and support your business.

## 3. I MAKE THE BEST OUT OF MY TIME

Make every moment count! Idle should never be in your vocabulary.

## 4. I KNOW WHO I AM

Take time to discover who you are as a person. Don't leave it up to people to tell you who you are.

## 5. I AM TOUCHING MY PURPOSE DAILY

Make sure a day doesn't go by where you are not doing something that has to do with your purpose.

## 6. I'M IN THE RIGHT PLACE, AT THE RIGHT TIME, TALKING TO THE RIGHT PEOPLE

It's important to connect with the right people, and the best way to do that is to find the place where they are.

## 7. I LIVE A LIFE OF INTEGRITY

It's important that you keep your word, as people don't want to do business with people they don't trust.

## 8. OPPORTUNITIES ARE ALWAYS AVAILABLE TO ME

Always look for ways to create and take advantage of opportunities for yourself and others.

## 9. I AM TEACHABLE

Never assume that you know everything, it pays to listen to people. They know more than you think they do.

## 10. I AM DEDICATED TO A LIFE OF EXCELLENCE

Make sure your life and actions reflect that of excellence, not perfection. Always strive to be better than you were yesterday.

# About the Authors

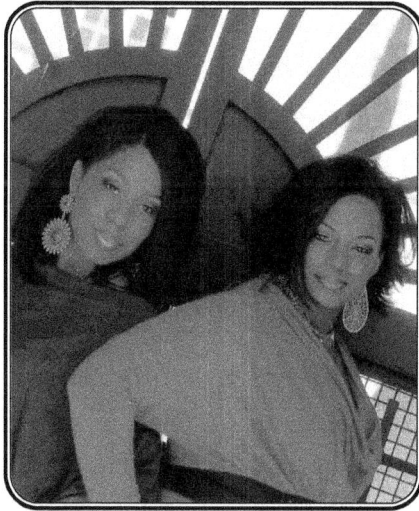

**Aletha Warren (on the right)**

Aletha is an expert coach, mentorship facilitator, and trainer. She provides tools and creates atmospheres where all the levels of an organization are involved in finding common ground and creating a work place, as well as a future, that they are committed to.

Ms. Warren is experienced in working with all levels of organizations, from entry-level employees to corporate leaders, balancing the human work experience with the bottom line. She specializes in collaborating with clients for win/win solutions in the areas of strategic thinking/planning and implementation, organizational learning, culture change, team and cross-team development, diversity inclusion, executive coaching, and leadership development. She is as comfortable using analytical and quantitative processes for decision-making as she is connecting with clients on a personal level to assess and manage the roots and sources of their challenges.

Intentionally choosing a variety of clients and industries, Ms. Warren brings acumen from broad-based experiences. In the not-for-profit arena, she has had the pleasure of teaching at Community Development Corporations as well as Religious Seminaries. Ms. Warren has facilitated small as well as large-scale mentoring events and has also spent several years as a group leader and trainer at Patten University. She has been an independent leadership consultant since 2001 and an internal trainer for many years. She has also recently completed her College degree with an emphasis in business from Oral Roberts University.

Ms. Warren continues her development in order to innovate and be an asset to her clients. She constantly scans the horizon for developing trends and the best practices while creating tailor-made solutions. Ms. Warren's other areas of expertise include certification in Leadership Coaching and Business.

Ms. Warren credits God for her success and accomplishments in life. She believes that He has given us all the ability and tools we need in order to have a successful life. "My job is to identify [the] tools, dust them off, and help put them into use until that person becomes a master at their craft." Her motto? "No more delay!"

### Tiffany C. Watkins

As a personal development specialist and master mentor, Tiffany C. Watkins regularly speaks at seminars and conferences, and also facilitates "Success" workshops. She has a strong passion to assist men and women in the empowerment areas of wholeness, wellness, success, spirituality, and balance. She is described as "an outstanding contributor" to the personal development industry and is a dynamic inspirational speaker as well as vocalist.

Tiffany possesses an encompassing passion for music and this same quality is seen in her ability to capture her listeners' attention, thus directing them to new levels of self-discovery and success.

Tiffany C. Watkins is the model of a woman living out her vision and purpose while demonstrating it with passion. She has achieved many landmark goals and accolades. She is an educator, motivational speaker, learned songstress, entrepreneur, trainer, master mentor, and has also been the recipient of numerous awards.

Ms. Watkins is a life-long learner who openly shares that her path to success was greatly initiated by reading numerous books, attending countless seminars, workshops, and courses, listening to thousands of hours of audio programs, as well as by attending many seminars and conferences for spiritual enlightenment. Her enthusiasm for continual learning and growth is commendable.

Eventually, through her years of study at Oral Roberts University and search for answers, Tiffany identified a range of reoccurring principles that unusually successful and wealthy people consistently implement. She made it her aim to uncover the most important principles for creating wealth, success, happiness, wholeness, and a life of balance.

She tirelessly learned and mastered these key principles and techniques, testing their soundness and authenticity by applying them to her own life first. She readily confesses that Kingdom Principles rebuilt her life from the ground up, making her who she is today. And after proving the success formula contained within the perfect Law of Liberty, she has taken the essential Biblical strategies that maximize success and significance within the Kingdom of God, and built a no-limits life for herself, her ministry, and her family.

Tiffany's mission as a life coach, personal development specialist, and mentor, is to share and teach others breakthrough-success principles by providing regular workshops, motivational speeches, training and mentoring programs through the V.I.P. Mentorship Program.

# Bibliography

- "African Lions, African Lion Pictures, African Lion Facts, African Cats-National Geographic." *National Geographic*. National Geographic Society. Web. http://animals.nationalgeographic.com/animals/mammals/african-lion/.
- "Agatha Christie" Wikipedia: The Free Encyclopedia. Web. http://en.wikipedia.org/wiki/Agatha_Christie
- "American Bald Eagle Information" Web. http://www.baldeagleinfo.com/eagle/eagle-facts.html
- *Chameleons*. 2002. Web. http://www.chameleonsonline.com.
- "Eagle." *Wikipedia: The Free Encyclopedia*. 14 July 2011. Web. http://en.wikipedia.org/wiki/eagle.
- Hauser, Mark. "The 25 Greatest Athletes of All Time". 26 February 2009. Web. http://bleacherreport.com/articles/130288-the-25-greatest-athletes-of-all-time
- Hawes, Larry. "Data and Statistics without Source Information Are Useless. *Together, We Can!* Wordpress, 16 Jan. 2011. Web http://lehawes.wordpress.com/2011/01/06/data-and-statistics-without-source-information-are-useless/.
- "Jackson, Michael" Wikipedia: The Free Encyclopedia. Web. http://en.wikipedia.org/wiki/Michael_Jackson

- "Presley, Elvis". Wikipedia: The Free Encyclopedia. Web. http://en.wikipedia.org/wiki/Elvis_Presley
- Stevens, Patsy. "Helen Keller". *Garden of Praise.* 2001. Web. http://gardenofpraise.com/ibdkell.htm.
- "Who Invented the First Computer?" Enotes. 9 October, 2011. Web. http://www.enotes.com/history/q-and-a/who-invented-first-personal-computer-288815
- "Wonder, Stevie" NNDB:Tracking the entire world. Web. http://www.nndb.com/people/535/000022469/
- Bible

# Quotes

"Aletha Warren's character leaks honesty and integrity is a core value that she consistently demonstrates. For her, challenges are inspiration, and difficulties are gracefully embraced. Ms. Warren is outfitted for just about any task that could find her.

Tiffany C. Watkins' successful ability to develop others is a direct result of her transparency and dedication to people regardless of age, diversity, or assignment. With a seemingly endless skill set, Tiffany places her equity in knowing the people around her and supporting them with humility and honor."

**Pastor Calvin Battle**
**CEO & Founder**
**Destiny Center in OK**

"Tiffany C. Watkins and Aletha Warren love people. Their heart is to see people succeed and to walk in their God-given destiny. Their ability to equip, encourage, and empower others is second to none".

**Jeremy Foster**
**The Jeremy Foster Show**
**Founder/Pastor of Hope City in TX**

"Tiffany Candyce Watkins has been a vibrant speaker on the subjects of self esteem, life strategies, developing ambition, vision, identity, and purpose. The professional singer/ songwriter has been referred to as a "dream resurrector", and has been successful in teaching many how to plot out their dreams using reasonable, and achievable goals for executing them. Her hands-on approach to coaching her students on realizing their life and business goals, has her rolling up her sleeves as she teaches by example. Tiffany's refreshing views as written in this book can be applicable to many facets of one's personal life and business."

**Taisha Dora**
**Former Senior Executive for International Wireless**
**Company**

"The VIP program has changed our lives forever, not only have we learned practical skills of everyday living but these leaders put us on track with following our dreams. This program is for anyone who has a desire to walk out their destiny and fulfill it. We will never be the same."

**Ryan & Cristina Baker**
**V.I.P. Clients**

If you have a drive which needs to be awakened, look no more. VIP is the push you need. VIP has changed my life, my perspective and my career.

**Desi Rodgers**
**V.I.P. Client**

V.I.P. greatly impacted my life, I was struggling with knowing what the plan was for my life and this program was a God send. V.I.P. helped me get on the right track. They taught me life principles and challenged me to apply them to my life. This program was used to help get me in line with my purpose. I am forever grateful to them.

**Darell Davis**
**V.I.P. Client**

# Bonus:
# V.I.P. Book of Daily Affirmations

*Business Affirmations*

1. My business is prosperous and operates at an optimal level of Success.
2. My employees/clients/team are the best of the best, they operate and deliver with excellence.
3. I use wisdom in all my decisions regarding myself, family, career and friends.
4. I am in complete purpose and people go out of their way to help me.
5. I am in the right place at the right time to meet the right connections.
6. I am confident, secure, and well versed in my business affairs.
7. Knowledge, money, influence, affluence and wealth chases, finds and attaches itself to me.
8. I learn and speak the language of the wealthy, elite, influential, affluent and business minded.
9. My understanding of business is increased to accommodate the level of wealth and business I will operate in.
10. I am quick to hear, slow to speak and slow to anger.

*Self-Esteem Affirmations*

1. I do NOT allow what people think of me to have power over me.
2. I like everything about me, my looks, my body, my personality, and I deserve love.
3. I am the epitome of excellence and discipline.
4. I am valuable to myself and others.
5. What I have to say matters, I am powerful!
6. I have intellectual creativity, wisdom and confidence.
7. My progress and destiny are not hindered by my words or anyone else's words.
8. I do not operate in dishonesty in any of my dealings.
9. I have the strength and courage to deal with any obstacle or set-back that comes my way.
10. I am not fearful or afraid of anyone or anything

*Financial Affirmations*

1. I am a great steward of my finances.
2. I am blessed because I give back to my community.
3. I have more than enough and function at an optimal level of financial intelligence.
4. I invest wisely.
5. I am a money magnet.
6. I only invest my time and finances in things that give me a lucrative return.
7. I am a financial guru in my own right.
8. I make money while I sleep.
9. I am financially independent.
10. I am debt-free.

*Affirmations for Singles*

1. I enjoy my singleness.
2. Singleness is not a disease, but an opportunity to explore who I am and what I like.
3. I am a whole and complete individual.
4. I do not settle for less than the best of everything.
5. I release all hurt and pain from past experiences and relationships.
6. All my relationships adds value to me.
7. I marry God's best for my life.
8. I am alone, but not lonely.
9. I am becoming what I'm looking for in a mate.
10. I am a successful single person.

*Leadership Affirmations*

1. My ability to serve others makes me a great leader.
2. I am a great communicator.
3. I am constantly improving and developing my skills as a leader.
4. I speak and think with eloquence, articulation and clarity.
5. As a leader, I operate in emotional intelligence.
6. People follow me because I am a great leader.
7. I inspire people to think outside the box.
8. I was born for greatness.
9. My experiences, good and bad, help to shape me into the leader I am today.
10. I am competent and confident in leadership strategies that bring results.

## Future\Present Spouse Affirmations

1. I love and am in love with my mate.
2. I honor and respect my covenant and vows I took in the sight of God.
3. My mate is my best friend.
4. I work daily at my marriage to make it successful.
5. I walk in love, forgiveness and understanding.
6. My household has an atmosphere of peace.
7. I communicate with clarity and wisdom when addressing an issue with my spouse.
8. I accept my mate's strengths and weaknesses and do not judge them.
9. I do not emotionally or physically tie myself to anyone other than my mate. Divorce is not an option.
10. I will speak, maintain, and feed my mate intellectually, socially, spiritually, soulishly and physically.

## Success Affirmations

1. I attract success and prosperity everywhere I go.
2. All of my plans and ideas lead me straight to success.
3. My inner circle is comprised of successful people.
4. Anything and everything I touch becomes successful.
5. My success and achievements open doors for me and cause me to be in places I've never been before.
6. My success is not measured by what I have, but who I am.
7. My success will leave a legacy for my children and children's children.
8. My attitude determines my altitude.
9. Success starts and ends with me.

10. Success is not how much money I make, but what type of impact I make.

*Love Affirmations*

1. I love and accept myself and others.
2. Confidence speaks. Integrity sings. Love shouts.
3. I love people and go out of my way to help them.
4. I am loved and deserve to be loved.
5. My love compels others to change.
6. My love draws the right people to my life.
7. I give and receive love freely, but wisely.
8. I still believe in the purity of true love.
9. Love always finds a way.
10. Love heals.

*Health Affirmations*

1. My body functions in optimal health.
2. I eat healthy.
3. I move my body at least 30 minutes a day.
4. Sickness and disease do not occupy my body.
5. My mind, body, and soul is healthy.
6. I will live a long, healthy life.
7. My body recovers and heals quickly.
8. My body gets the correct vitamins and nutrients it needs to operate on a daily basis.
9. I discipline my body daily.
10. Health is my portion.

## Emotional Intelligence Affirmations

1. I am a wise steward of my emotions.
2. I have control over my emotions, my emotions do not have control over me.
3. I know how to identify my emotional state and take the necessary steps to stabilize them.
4. I do not think or make decisions based on my emotions.
5. My emotional balance brings healthy stability to my life.
6. I daily become more aware of my emotions.
7. I acknowledge all of my emotions, but choose to hold on to the positive ones.
8. I master my emotions daily.
9. I do not allow people to have power over my emotional state.
10. I am in tune with my emotions.

## Peace Affirmations

1. I choose peace and serenity.
2. I work and live in a peaceful environment.
3. I follow peace in every situation.
4. I am calm and peaceful in the midst of chaos.
5. My home is a place of peace.
6. Peace follows me everywhere I go.
7. I am a peacemaker in any situation.
8. I embody peace.
9. My peace is worth fighting for.
10. My heart follows peace.

*Affirmations for Men*

1. I am a King.
2. I am a confident man that knows who I am and know what I want.
3. I am a man that takes care of my responsibilities.
4. I am a man who embodies great integrity.
5. I am a man who is socially aware, and intellectually adept.
6. I am a man of excellence.
7. I find my wife in excellent timing and we are compatible.
8. I believe in myself
9. I am a man who is not afraid of commitment.
10. Life's challenges will only make me stronger.

*Affirmations for Women*

1. I am a woman of confidence and elegance.
2. I am a wise woman who takes care of her responsibilities.
3. I am a woman of integrity and grace.
4. I am a Queen.
5. I am a woman of excellence.
6. I am a woman who empowers other women
7. I am a woman who is healthy socially, physically, emotionally, psychologically, and spiritually.
8. I am a woman of beauty, class and presence.
9. I am a woman of value and I know my worth.
10. I am a woman who is confident, and walks in purpose.

# Note from the Authors

The goal of Access Granted: The V.I.P. Principal is to get you moving in the direction that causes life to come alive, your heart to beat for purpose, and your dreams to awaken through action. Action is the movement that causes life to happen for you, to you, and through you. It is our desire that you are motivated to the point of action, which will cause your life to look different. By applying these principals, you will begin to see your life change for the better.

There are no limits to your life. If you see limitations, revisit some of the pages in this book. The only limits are the ones that you place on yourself. Life is open to you, no matter your age, nationality, background, or situation. Take it by the reins. You have the power. You have the instructions. Take it, VIP. Take it to the top. We'll see you there.

Executive Life Coaches,
Aletha Warren & Tiffany C. Watkins

www.ingramcontent.com/pod-product-compliance
Lightning Source LLC
LaVergne TN
LVHW021358080426
835508LV00020B/2334